SESAME STREET

All about NURSES

Brianna Kaiser

Lerner Publications ◆ Minneapolis

Who Are the People in Your Neighborhood?

Sesame Street has always been set smack in the middle of a friendly, busy community. We know that for all children, getting to know their communities is crucially important. So is understanding that everyone in the neighborhood—including kids!—has a part to play. In the *Sesame Street®ₐ Loves Community Helpers* books, *Sesame Street*'s favorite furry friends help young readers get to know some of these helpers better.

Sincerely,
The Editors at
Sesame Workshop

Table of Contents

Let's Meet Nurses!

Nurses are terrific! They help me and my family stay healthy.

Why We Love Nurses

Nurses help people all over the community. They work in doctor's offices, hospitals, and schools.

The nurse always makes me feel better.

Some nurses wear special clothing called scrubs. Scrubs come in fun colors and patterns.

My favorite scrubs are the ones with rubber duckies on them.

People see nurses at doctor's offices for checkups. Nurses check the patient's temperature, height, and weight.

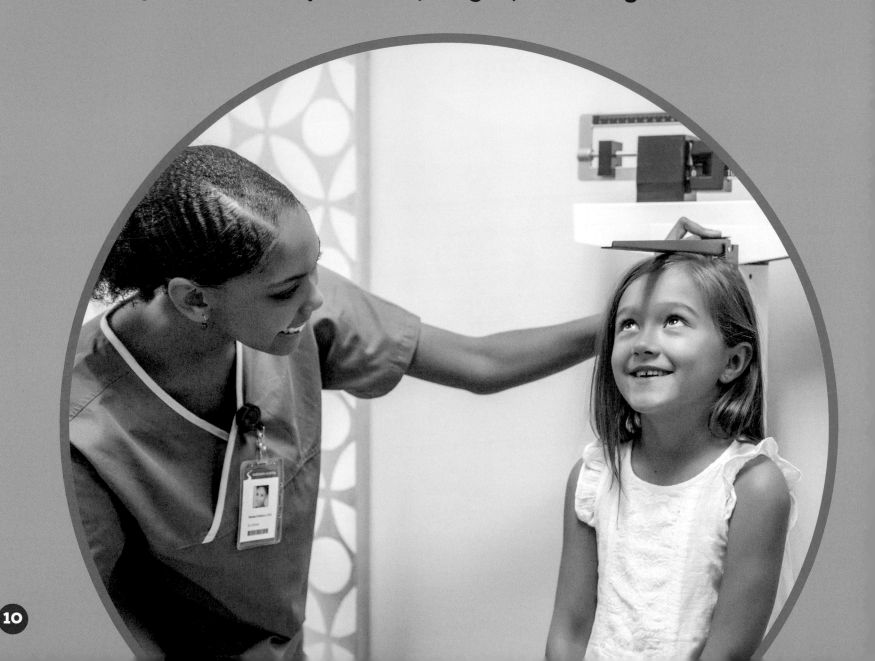

I hope that scale is big enough for my garbage can.

Nurses keep records of patients. Nurses look at a patient's records when they see them. They keep track of a person's health.

Nurses can see if I grew since my last visit.

I ask my nurse how to take care of a sore throat.

Nurses talk to patients about how they're feeling.

They ask a lot of questions and take notes.
They also answer patients' questions.

School nurses help students stay healthy.
Students visit the school nurse if they don't feel well.

Elmo goes to the nurse when his tummy hurts.

Students go to the nurse if they get hurt.
They also go if they need medicine.

The nurse gives me a bandage.

Sometimes people have to go to the hospital.
Nurses help give them extra care.

Nurses know what patients need.

21

Some nurses focus on one type of care. Nurses may work in the emergency room or help deliver babies.

You can always count on a nurse, *ah ah ah!*

Nurses care for their patients.
They comfort them when they are upset.

Me nurse always nice!

Nurses also take patients to and from tests.

Nurses make communities better. They take care of people no matter how old they are or where they live.

Nurses are heroes!

Thank You, Nurses!

Now it's your turn! Write a thank-you note to your favorite nurse.

Dear Nurse,

Thank you for taking care of me when I visit you. You help me stay healthy!

Your friend,

Ji-Young

Picture Glossary

checkups: visits to the doctor to check on your health

patient: a person who visits a nurse or a doctor

records: information about someone's health

scrubs: clothing worn by nurses, doctors, and other health-care workers

Read More

Murray, Julie. *Nurses*. Minneapolis: Abdo Kids Junior, 2021.

Unwin, Cynthia. *Meet a Nurse!* New York: Children's Press, 2021.

Waxman, Laura Hamilton. *Nurse Tools*. Minneapolis: Lerner Publications, 2020.

Index

Photo Acknowledgments

Image credits: FS Productions/Getty Images, pp. 4, 10; Ariel Skelley/DigitalVision/Getty Images, p. 5; ER Productions Limited/DigitalVision/Getty Images, pp. 6, 22; FatCamera/iStock/Getty Images, pp. 7, 14, 15, 16, 30 (patient); Rachel Frank/Corbis/Getty Images, p. 8; Terry Vine/DigitalVision/Getty Images, pp. 9, 23 (right), 29, 30 (scrubs); JGI/Jamie Grill/Getty Images, p. 11; SDI Productions/E+/Getty Images, pp. 12, 24, 27, 30 (record); Rick Gomez/Getty Images, pp. 13, 30 (checkup); milatas/Shutterstock.com, p. 17; Jamie Grill/The Image Bank/Getty Images, p. 18; Steve Hix/Fuse/Corbis/Getty Images, p. 19; Fuse/Corbis/Getty Images, p. 20; Ridofranz/Getty Images, p. 21; sturti/E+/Getty Images, p. 23 (left); monkeybusinessimages/iStock/Getty Images, p. 25; Courtney Hale/E+/Getty Images, p. 26.

Cover: Pressmaster/Shutterstock.com.

To my mom, my all-time favorite nurse. Thank you, Nurse MK!

Lerner Publications Company
An imprint of Lerner Publishing Group, Inc.
241 First Avenue North
Minneapolis, MN 55401 USA

For reading levels and more information, look up this title at www.lernerbooks.com.

Main body text set in Mikado Medium.
Typeface provided by HVD Fonts.

Designer: Mary Ross

Library of Congress Cataloging-in-Publication Data

Names: Kaiser, Brianna, 1996- author.
Title: All about nurses / Brianna Kaiser.
Description: Minneapolis : Lerner Publications , [2023] | Series: Sesame street ® loves community helpers | Includes bibliographical references and index. | Audience: Ages 4–8 | Audience: Grades K–1 | Summary: "Nurses are an essential part of every community. The lovable characters from Sesame Street teach readers how nurses care for their patients and keep us all healthy"—Provided by publisher.
Identifiers: LCCN 2021036040 | ISBN 9781728456119 (library binding) | ISBN 9781728463780 (paperback) | ISBN 9781728462141 (ebook)
Subjects: LCSH: Nurses—Juvenile literature. | Nursing—Juvenile literature.
Classification: LCC RT61.5 .K35 2023 | DDC 610.73—dc23

LC record available at https://lccn.loc.gov/2021036040

Manufactured in the United States of America
1-50681-50100-1/25/2022